Chalk-dust

- Collected poems -

1987 - 2023

Thanks to Kindle Direct – without which...etc etc

'There was chalk-dust!'

- John McEnroe

*'Keep your eyes on that far-distant star,
and the sun's gonna shine where you are'*

- John Stewart – 'Omaha rainbow'

Chalk-dust represents the majority of the poems
written by myself over the period 1987 to 2023.
A number of new poems written in late 2023 are included,
together with some poems from a humorous collection
entitled *'Say no more'.*

Hope you enjoy.

PS. - October 2023

Poems

Phoenix Park in Snow

Those dark-coated figures sliding
Down a snow-blanked papal cross hill
A half-mile from where I'm standing,
The shrieks of delight come shrill

Across the white expanse of an afternoon
Dark of tree-line and cloud-scape still,
And the timeless word I'm looking for
Comes like a cross-word; - *Brueghel*!

- 2010 -

Lahinch

for Florence & Lorna

Aren't you glad I took it now?
- Took that snap picture
In the high winds
With those background waves
All white and driven,
Spraying the promenade
Above the stony banks,
- Took that snap picture
Of you, with your hair
All tossed and astray
And holding the buggy tight,
But the child's face
Only lit with sheer delight.

-1995 -

A pint of Dublin

Old misty-eyed myopic Jim
Let's play a trick on him!
As the barman wipes spilt froth
From the polished brass of the table-top
And calls '*last orders now!*',
There'll be one for the road for Jim,
Just imagine the face of him!
When we salt and pepper his pint
Before he turns back around
And starts to sing or something,
Or reaches for his accordion.
Drink it up Jim, knock it back in one!
Enjoy your one-for-the-road,
Enjoy your pint of Dublin!

- 1991 -

Great Juggernauts heading West

Economic activity is measured out
In those sodium-soaked kilometres,
In the strings of light disembodied
By drenching rain or freezing fog,

By Juggernauts ploughing east and west,
Leviathans - blind and relentless
Towards wholesale warehouses
And supermarket deadlines;

At 4 a.m. on insomniac nights
They sweep by, over the high wall,
In split seconds gone.
Silence then, nothing following.

- 1997 -

The Egg-man of Balgaddy

Were you ever, ever, egged
By the Egg-man of *Balgaddy?*

The little bollix who lobbed an egg
Hitting the side-window of my car,

Just an overweight kid in a dirty tracksuit
Several sizes too large

Before dancing off in celebratory triumph
Through his rained-on grimy estate

Like some self-styled local hero,
- He's not famous or anything,

In truth he is not even known
As 'The Egg-man of Balgaddy?'

I've merely thought that up,
But some day - who knows? - he might be,

And I can claim I too was egged
By 'The Egg-man of Balgaddy'.

- 2005 -

Greystones

for Florence

Greystones, by the sea-front
At *Spendlove's* terraced café,
Sun shining like the fourth of July
And I took a digital photo of you
Just as a sun-cloud came over
Quenching all the yellows and blues
And putting the grey into *Greystones*
And that back-drop of harbour view.
Now I'm waiting again for the sun
But not as it happens for long,
My dear – permission for me to take
Just one more picture of you?

- 4/7/2013 -

And yet the planes fly

You can drown in daylight air,
Resuscitate on the sea-bed,
'Love dangles by a thread'
Like the *Crosby-Nash* song said,

And yet the planes still fly,
It's no mundane miracle,
Launch their tonnage into the sky
For destinations invisible,

And you do what you must do
Whether beg borrow or steal,
You do what you must do
To re-invent the wheel,

And someday you too will fly,
To this magic dance you're fated,
Someday to a stranger smile
'It's complicated'.

- 1994 -

If you're going…

I went to San Francisco
Hung out by Union Square,
I headed for *Haight & Ashbury*
But saw no hippies there,

No vestige of the sixties' dream
No '*make love not war*',
I stood on the sidewalk then
Until I wondered what-for

Amid corporate office-blocks
And the suits and brief-cases
Of fast-walking executives
With murderous faces.

- 1988 -

The Book

for Arthur Janov

You idly browse in *Veritas*
To spot at random a book
- One you have never seen before,
Which - after timeless minutes -
You place back on the shelf,
Until some revolt in the self
Compels you pick up again

And read a little more,
Then more, then more again.
And now you cannot leave this book,
You know at least this much,
- That by hook or by crook
You must take this book,
Into your life already changing.

- 1987 -

Strands

Summer skies and rented caravans
And what I remember most
Were the strands, - at *Enniscrone*
Striding like an Olympian,

Or *Barna* - and the Silver Strand's
Chest-high anaesthetic swells
That left us salt-sensed and shivering
And running for sun-dried towels,

Or that tide at *Spanish Point*
Raging in with spray and burst
Like it meant business,
I willed it on to do its worst.

Rosslare – that final year
Wondering, all mind-at-sea,
And my mother, waiting there,
With Sunday papers on a deck-chair

Bemused, perplexed, demanding
What on God's earth had kept me?

- 2000 -

Connolly's Folly

Old and centuried, the damp cut-stone
Of its high arches and central edifice,
It's high pillar phallic and dizzying at noon,
At dusk, an imposing motif over treetops
Decorated by crows, the ground gravelled
And security-fenced now where surely once
Were garden parties long since past all recall,
Pasture fields surround, the whole pile left
To circling birds or odd infrequent visitor
Lured on a whim from the nearby motor-way.

- 2013 -

Eine Lange Nacht

Only once in my life have I been without a bed
Due to failing to advance-book a *Jungendherberge*
In Munich in 1980 with the men's hostel full
In the *Haupt-Banhoff* a Turk invited me to Istanbul
Reckoning maybe I looked a little too lonely
I checked the red-cross – women & children only,
I tried to kip then in a plastic waiting-room seat
Before security with Alsatians on their 2 a.m. beat
Came ankle-tapping the tramps and none too gently
I moved on – found a bus-shelter eventually
Where a sad-faced Spaniard came presently by
With a body-language suggesting some sexual try
So I moved on again, got way out of there
Toured the street-lights in the cold pre-dawn air
Until, at first light, the Banhoff would open again,
And the hard plastic seats a sight more welcome.

Something Happened

Something Happened by Joseph Heller
I had it right there in my bedroom locker
Ready to read, for it to disappear,
The culprit was my mother - I fear,
Deeming it unsuitable for some un-named reason
Though nothing would be said of this petty treason,
So – it's a book I've never quite got to read
Because of that over-maternalistic deed
But I've read somewhere the novel's narrator
Alludes to some problem with *his* mother….

Fresh Evidence

i.m. Rory Gallagher

Walking wounded?
Some nights nothing else will do
But to stick on *Fresh Evidence*
And wallow in the volume
Of that famed Fender
Grunge guitar grinding,
With Rory roaring
Through and through;
You've done your damage
I've had…. enough of you!

- 1995 -

Not quite a Picasso

The jigsaw was fun for a while,
The jigsaw that was 'us',
The jigsaw that was really two jigsaws,
Collage fragments of past jigsaws,
That fragmented our even smiles,

Your tequila sunrise verandas
Against my clouded maudlin sky?
Our horizons forever out of synch,
Perspectives that were never- quite-right,
The jigsaw was fun for a while.

- 1989 -

Dreaming of a Shore

I know now what you were trying to do;
You were trying to blow me out of the water,
Out of my smug life-boat
To make me drown or swim
'Like everyone has to swim'

I watched your shots fall short, go over
My head and wide, make meaningless splashes
In the choppy distance,
I held onto my pathetic life-boat,
I kept on dreaming of a shore.

- 1999 -

Keem bay, Achill

(for David)

Afterwards I would blame the wet-suit
For my clumsiness, my out-of-sorts
As the Atlantic breakers rolled in
Enough to power up a power-station!
For I was cluttered in that dolphin-like skin,
That was warm - but it's buoyancy rendering
Me as flotsam in the strength of the wave,
A hapless *Sancho* towards my companion Dave
In his own skin a natural knight of the sea,
Who afterwards would put it succinctly
In his time-honoured quipped persiflage
'Un petit contretemps avec la mer sauvage?'

- Sept 2011 -

Sol

As morning becomes noon
The tall side facades
Of the *Torremolinos* towers
Shed their shadows for the sun,

Arid hills beyond
High and heat-hazed
Shimmer
Like a spaghetti western

As, breakfasted and done,
From a samba-blasting minaret
(disguised as a palm tree)
Sun-seekers are called to worship.

- 2010 -

The Carnival

Over the fields and high hedge-rows
The brightly-painted carnival
Tilts its shapes against the sky,
It is an invitation and we go
Picking our way over the muddy path,
You will happily choose the roller-coaster
Whilst I will gravitate towards the ghost-train
(Life being roller-coaster enough for me)
Wherein I will defiantly give the fingers
To those leering lit-up spectres
And delight in the déjà vu,
But you will not take that ghost-train
Nor chance to explore the mirror-hall
To '*see yourself as never before*!'
Though I've purchased the tickets for two.
Chalk it down to the imponderable,
We will compromise with The Waltzer,
You will laugh, I'll go green and dizzy
- Though what I really wanted to do
(We have differing fears its true
And skip the Madame's predictions)
Was to ride on that ghost-train with you.

A no-good Place

When the head bottle-washer of the rumour mill
Has zoned in on your case,
And the whooping cowboys band together
Smelling the blood of the chase,
Don't be too surprised
To learn the Sheriff is compromised,
Just plan ahead, get out of town,
Hit the mountains before sundown,
Leaving no horse-shoe track, no trace,
Keep a straight face like a Poker game,
Water that horse, change your name,
Check your saddle, your shoe-lace,
Get the hell out of that no-good place.

- 2003 -

Gold

(for Catherine)

When you ran those thirty yards
At your top sprinting speed
Towards the trolley-bay
Outside the *Supermarche*
Not stopping at all until
You hit the finish of my arms
And I had to turn full circle
To take your hurtled weight…
I thought of it just now,
- Of this impromptu field event,
And place it now and forever
In the podium of memory;
Of you at four years old
And how casually the Gods
Surely awarded us that day
'In the combined category
- Olympic gold'.

- 2003 -

A dream of Cricket

All hell and horror and hammering;
Hangover doesn't help, rats aboard
The golden lifeboat clambering,

Dear God – battery's flat, and yet
I know I dreamt, for I woke
With a fine appreciation of cricket!

Forsooth! – the game just clicked with me,
A-shifting of some cosmic scoreboard
By that bowler and batsman symmetry,

When the myth of the phoenix seemed lost,
Where boulders won't get shifted
Or coin of chance get tossed,

And the past a cracked mirror of imperfect grace.
And the future not what it used to be,
Yet I dreamt, divined such a place

Where bat belts ball to a skywards spin,
Out for a photo-finish or a boundary!
- Such small great things to believe in.

- 1997 -

Remember too

…in this time-stressed world
Of rat-race indifference
There is also a beauty;
- Like that random woman's
Disarming ever-polite '*sorry*'
When she bumped into me
With her supermarket trolley…

Hold that memory - don't lose it
Or allow be over-written
By some remembered sneer
Or crude crowd-fuelled jeer;
In this unthinking world
Of rat-race indifference
Remember the beauty too.

- 2016 -

Terrible Hair

Yes, that's me there
On a school tour
Aged seventeen
Atop the *Eiffel Tower,*
1978 and terrible hair!
Smiling ear to ear
And all the city of Paris
Stretched in a dazzle below.
You'd never diagnose
Anything in particular
From that mile-wide
For-the-camera smile,
Only terrible hair,
Though here, just now,
Aeons into the future
I'm realizing that's the guy,
Inarticulate, self-doubting,
Naïve, un-debonair,
(Survivalist extraordinaire!)
With terrible hair,
- That that's the guy
Who got me here.

- 2002 -

Allotment

I can see it yet, even now,
Those worn and baggy black trousers
And mud-dusted shoes,
And him, all red-faced and sweating
On a sultry afternoon at the allotment,

Enthusing on his potato drills,
All keyed up from honest spade-work
And now, sudden and unbidden,
Out of nowhere I recall
The blue rope and the tinder sticks

Where, with an effort, he stooped
To mark out his potato plot,
Where he was happiest,
Hammering and tamping them down
With the back-end of a spade,

Taking a breather then
Before remarking to no-one
'That's something done!'
As, stifling a guilty laugh
For I know I must have done…

- let me explain - I was his son.

- 1999 –

The General

Eyes shadowed under peaked cap,
He gives a stiff salute for flag and country,
His uniform decorated and impeccable,
His countenance carefully angled,
It is of love of country he speaks,
And of patriotic vision,
He will not name the enemy
For he weighs the value of words
Both spoken and unspoken,
And thousands will starve behind barbed fences,
Examples will be made, houses burnt,
The throats of every boy-child cut
And the perpetrators pose for photographs,
But no - not the General,
The General stands aloof
His gaze fixed beyond the farthest hills,
His portrait pride of place
In every respectable living room.

(referring to a photo of Ante Pavelic – Ustase leader)

Apple Tree

As soon as he woke up there in his bed
He knew he'd been dreaming about the universe
- that vastness he could not get his head around,
Its emptiness that could never be filled,
And he knew then what he needed, - an apple tree!
That he would grow from a single apple seed
To grow and expand and like the universe!
Already he could see it dominate his lawn
It's curious gnarled branches like knuckles
That reminded him of an ancient walking stick,
And kids tree-climbing like he once had done,
Apples too, hanging there - lots of them,
And then - on some damp December
He would witness from his window
An apple falling, thump onto wet grass,
The most natural thing in the universe.

- 2014 -

Newfoundland

Aboard a wood and leather replica
of the sail-boat christened St. Brendan,
its crew with Captain *Severin*
on massive seas off Iceland
and deadly floes off Greenland,
sailing through doubts and silences
on gull-lonely waters…

A torn hull needed stitching
and barnacles - removing,
all to reach its destination
to prove the unprovable story
and so, prove all our stories;
- that we all might find Newfoundland!

- 2017 -

Watching the Storm

The ship's bow climbing in seeming slow motion,
Poised, sheer, on an ever-rising wall
Into nothing, only a green abyss of ocean
Awaits the inexorable plunging fall,
It is miles out on the Norwegian

Sea, and already another slow-rising mountain
Before the water-draped bow is hit
Full force, the bridge-camera shuddering,
(And yet – that voice-calm Captain), - and you?
- on full-screen You-tube, merely watching it!

No one can paint you!

Oh, they'll paint you, they'll paint you all right,
Exhibit you in thoughtless impressionistic
Brushstrokes,
Casually hang you in their hall of fools,
But then again
You can walk away, - look!
Merely to tread
Anonymously down that street
And not look back
Is to dance with gravity,
Is to spit in the eye of the great nada!
For who can paint you?
Like *Dorian Gray*
Cheap portraits may wilt and die
In redundant galleries.

- 1990 -

Initiation

How long for intangible truth to sink in?
For years a swept-aside rumour, a blur,
But always one eye on the ringside,
Time to walk out the dressing-room door
For the final initiation of senses,
Now doubled-up, knees down on the floor,

Time to feel the original stomach punch!
The almighty gut-spiller, and then
The crowd-hush and referee counting
Though never quite counting to ten…
Proof now – if proof was what you wanted,
Of the punch that won't throw you again.

-1994 -

Hope

Endgame approaches in the game of Chess
(My game-plan reduced to a tattered mess)
But I leave uncounted my options
(I tell myself there *are* options)
Despite mistakes and *the pressure, the pressure*,
Despite my defence's mile-wide fissure
Some philosophy must be cobbled together
Involving my solitary Pawn and whether
The straight-lined Bishop or chaotic Knight
Serves me best to keep things tight,
With my King un-castled and both Rooks gone
All now pinned on the humblest Pawn,
That, by some alchemy, some move unseen,
May yet convert to match-winning Queen!

First day of the world

It's the first day of the season,
First intimation of winter's bite,
Stepping out from central heating
Into a brilliant pristine light

Into chilled air finding throat and lung
From winds that have scoured the sky
And shaken clear the rain-clouds,
Leaves fallen, swept, scattered high.

Sphinx-like on a near shed roof
A cat lies impassively there,
Staring through to some beyond
Its eyes turned marble in the glare

(Like nature seeing with nature's eyes)
As Magpies erupt in the trees,
Sunlight painting the high rooftops,
Poplars shivering in the breeze,

So morning happens, absolute,
The flag of the day is unfurled,
What's gone before is mere history
On this, - first day of the world.

White Ship

An early stroll down an unfamiliar country road
All sun-shadowed tarmac, all ditch and tree,
Somewhat sun-raddled by a night of drink
Are my eyes playing tricks on me?

For a ship's prow passes, all shiny white,
Making me double-take at this absurdity!
High and looming, sailing through a field?
That was no field but a ditch-hidden estuary.

- Waterford, 2010 -

Forever

The muddied path frozen in the February air,
Mist frosting the deserted playing pitches
And the fields that run distant by trees and ditches,
Find yourself alone this early morning hour,

Where breath turns to vapour, just hanging there,
Under a grey-white impenetrable sky,
Dispersing like old arguments that may live or die,
Your unthinking wish is to walk this stretch forever.

- 2005 -

Behind Sun-shaded Avenidas

On a ramble down unfamiliar back-streets
Behind sun-shaded *Costa* Avenidas,
Drawn to the revving of motor-bikes
And soon I spot them – the motor-bikers,
On a patched of rubbled waste ground,
Helmetless, they play their improvised game
Of accelerating hard against a high wall
Before braking in the nick of time…
So - the spirit of *Don Quixote* lives
Or perhaps a vestige of the *Toreador*?
Behind off-beat *Torremolimos* Avenidas
They tilt their motorbikes at *la Muerte*.

- 2010 -

Second sight

On second sight
It was not an axe-wielding giant
But merely a windmill,

On second sight
It was not a discovery
But an oil-spill,

On second sight
He was no prophet
Just another fool-on-the-hill,

On second sight
It was pure lady-luck
Not 'power of the will',

On second sight
It was not a just war
But an overkill,

On second sight
It had nothing to do
With principle.

Half

i.m BMJ

He grumbles wryly
About his double bed half-empty
And I laugh
Knowing he is half joking,

He points through shabby curtains
Down onto the street
Remarks at the young student talent
Strolling under falls of rain

And I know what he's thinking
On his half-empty double bed,
And his life of half-chances
Halving now by the month,

And how he half exists
And maybe we all half-exist!
'It's all right for you' he says,
And I half laugh.

- 2001 -

Tracks

Listen!
Can you hear it?
Another train coming

Down the tunnel
(From past or future?)
Can you feel it?

Let it pass
Like other trains pass,
Shake us with temporary thunder,

Let it pass over
Without fuss or incident,
And it will pass

If we keep heads down,
Keep our formation,
Our parallel agreement.

- 1991 -

Inis Turk

A simple mix-up at the quay;
It was the wrong boat what we took
That took us out to *Inis Turk*
Where - no sooner had we landed
Than time to be back on our way,
Time only to eye its stone-pocked contours,
And the colonies of gulls and gannets
As the out-going ferry unslung
Its cargo of pallets and beer kegs,
Props for a good night to come.

And there we might well have stayed
- Bargained a lodging somewhere,
 But we were heading out and away
The ferry kicking in Atlantic swells,
But what I wanted to explain, to say
Was how that sea-borne mist descended
And how so rapidly it rendered
To a glimpsed outline in charcoal
The island where we might have stayed,
Withdrawing inexorably from the visible
In realms of blessed rain, ethereal
As our promise to return someday.

- 2008 -

Volcano

First nothing,
Or nothing much,
So it seemed,
Though some clumsy
Articulation
Was about to waken,

A pressure
Intolerable, too much,
Hot rock and ash
Firing furious
Beyond all
Will or control,

Earth's very sputum,
It's subterranean sickness rush,
Giving gurgled voice
No God nor Man
Could think to deny
Or shush.

When the Train comes

Enniscrone beach '76 – cloudless sunny skies
And a seascape stretched vast and infinite
As the future - as only a teenager's can be,
Any yet in your stomach – near-naked animal fear,
A credit then to *Sutherland Brothers & Quiver*
For that song on the transistor playing
when the train comes...ohh when the train comes...
That against all odds you could believe it -
- be waiting at the station, how about you?

- 1997 -

Our Heroes

Don Quixote
Dazed from his encounter
With the windmill,

And man-servant Sancho
The practical one
Dusting him off,

Does Don curse his own stupidity?
Does loyal Sancho
Stifle a laugh?

Seems not - they saddle up
Twin-headed still
By fantasy and foreboding,

Let's wish our heroes
The best for the road,
Their luck is our luck.

- 1994 -

Weighty Statues

Much is left invisible;
Nine-tenths of the iceberg
Lies underwater
That gives it balance
So its surface will not sway,
And you would not be you
If not for what you've been through
Yet how much we'd wish
Would all just melt away
That continuously must be swept
Under rug or cushion or gown
Or better best
Buried in the garden,
Weighty statues
Holding it down.

Different class

Out by *Seapoint* I take off my cap,
- My *San Diego* branded baseball cap,
And hold it in my hands,
Reading for the first time
It's label 'manufactured in China'.
I wipe the sweat off my scalp
With my *Made in China*
San Diego-branded baseball cap....

But - those white *sea-caps* racing
With the wild winds off the bay
Is quite another story!
- So entirely made
By different forces altogether.

- 3/5/2017 -

Let the tide wash up what it will

I throw my old half-baked poems away
For they've not much new to say,
In order to break new ground, to forget,
To embrace instead 'the immediate'
Will be the new intended philosophy,
Make *today* the epi-centre of reality!
- Or does that merely strait-jacket the mind?
Why even bother with the intellectual grind
In the first place? – oh hell!
Let the tide wash up what it will.

Our Brenda

You have to know our Brenda,
For if you did, you'd know
That she must sing *Crazy*
Because it's her last night
And everyone who knows her knows
She must sing *Crazy* tonight
- That *Crazy* is her song,
Though tonight the band is cookin'
On Brazilian jazz-tinged samba!
All tom-tom drums and nodding bass,
Guitar fingers all over the place,
They do not notice our Brenda
In the bustling crowd – but they will
Come hell or high water
When she finishes her *pina colada*
Under the *Praia da Oura* moon,
They will realize soon
She's got to sing her *Crazy*
And they will find the chords - they will
Because Brenda won't stop until…
And she's crazy for trying
Just crazy for trying
But crazy, *Crazy,* is her song.

- 1991 -

One for Tommy

What cruel casual law decreed,
What mindless lottery
Wheel of ill-fortune spun?
What cosmic sniper, drunken psycho
Firing into the crowd
Picked you out?
Could have picked anyone,

Teacher, Athlete, Enthusiast,
How you relished
The crack of the starting gun,
I want to tell you
About the municipal track
They laid out in Irishtown,
I want to tell you
About the lady's soccer game
In Ringsend park
Coach yelling on the side-line
On a breezy Saturday morning,
I want to tell you
How the wind hustled,
How the rain held off…

Our conversation is an imaginary one
But beyond that finish tape
Where the clocks are stopped
We'll have that drink
- There's surely a place
Some half-decent bar
In oblivion.

Everything must go!

In the tiny little corner-shop of hurt
Nothing's worth more than it's worth,
Buy a bottle of vintage poison wine
For as little as nineteen ninety-nine
Nothing's worth more than it's worth,

In the tiny little corner-shop of hurt
You'll find things though lost in the dirt
Perhaps a betrayal or some slice of treason,
Can we tempt you with a little un-reason?
But nothing's worth more than it's worth.

In the tiny little corner-shop of hurt
In shelves and corners and in every berth
The cheeky Charlies and the windup toys
Chant old rumours and not-quite-true lies,
 But nothing's worth more than it's worth.

In the tiny little corner-shop of hurt
Often dammed-up emotions pour forth,
A fossilized school-yard insult
Or gibe overheard as an adult
But nothing's worth more than it's worth.

In the tiny little corner-shop of hurt
There are nooks and crannies, no dearth
Of cowboys slinging such crass assumption,
Unkind memories lacking critical gumption,
Nothing's worth more than it's worth.

In the tiny little corner-shop of hurt
We regret we can't issue a cert
And every shop has its closing time so
There's a policy of 'everything must go'
Because nothing's worth more than it's worth.

In the tiny little corner-shop of hurt
Nothing's worth more than your shirt,
No refunds alas so better think twice,
You can haggle away but still pay the price
Though nothing's worth more than it's worth.

In the tiny little corner-shop of hurt
Find bargain-bins of what once cost the earth,
Feel free to browse but please don't delay
Tomorrow's peace of mind can be purchased today
Nothing's worth more than it's worth.

In the tiny little corner-shop of hurt
From Shanghai to Palookaville to Perth
It's not what you want but what you need
Herbal remedies – albeit unguaranteed
Unlikely worth more than they're worth.

Turbulence

That's what you get sometimes
Six miles above the Atlantic;
Risking a remark on turbulence
To a next-sitting unknown passenger

And receiving the frostiest of glares
As if the mention of turbulence
Was a breaking of unwritten rules,

As if, turbulent or not
I had no right to intrude
On her silence, her turbulence!

Dear stranger, merely rude,
I agree our turbulences are incomparable,
That my turbulence is not your turbulence,

That its best our turbulences never meet,
Though unbeknownst, you've sent me
Into a headfirst spin of memory,

O what storms you've precipitated in my head
By eyes that have said 'drop dead'
But watch me tilt my camouflaged wings
And tilt away over mountain and glacier,
Watch me – I'm an expert Arctic flier.

The Western Camera-man

Through the Western camera lens
Small pigeons of hope appear to flutter
In the young prisoner's eyes
Who stands accused of 'un-Islamic activity',

In this rare access to notorious *Evin* prison
Small pigeons of hope flutter briefly
Only to be extinguished;
For the Western Camera-man
Is only that; - the Western Camera-man.

- 1995 -

Top Gun

Bunch of hooded Arabs
Running down a street
Bunch of Hooded Arabs
In the shit-hole heat
Disguised as women,
Disguised as children
Chucky's got the ten-four
To take 'em out,
Can't take any chances,
Can't be any doubt,
For it's all been simulated
On new-gen battle-zone
And when that baby goes
O Boy! - those running suckers
Will get blasted right back
Beyond the age of stone.
Bunch of hooded Arabs
Running down a street
Repeat!
Bunch of hooded Arabs
Look like in retreat
Situation normal!
Chucky's got the big ten-four!
Bunch of hooded Arabs
No more.

- 1995 -

Dog

Walking alone along the sea-shore
Where others walk their dogs
And already here's one now, unleashed,
Gangly, bounding and unbounded
To make a general nuisance of itself,
Ears pricked and poised, nose-curious,
With no conception of boundaries
Or other new-age constructs
Like personal space – are you kidding!
This time it's merely sniffing,
Looks like you passed the test! – already
It's forgotten all about you
And moving on – readily distracted
By some wrack caught-up in seaweed
Or those playful charging sea-waves
It can't quite get its doggy head around.

- 2017 -

Sunglasses - L.A.

(for Sean and David)

Mid-March and merely in the nineties
Though somehow you don't sweat a drop
In the post-card blue - shorts and tee-shirt will do

And sunglasses – you gotta wear sunglasses,
You can be anyone in L.A. with sunglasses,
Down on Venice, or the Kings Head, Santa
Monica,

It helps, confidence is the second currency,
Goes a long way, like with Davy at the bar
In that stand-out Dylanesque jacket

Exchanging hi-fives with every passing shaded
dude,
As two blonds stood there mystified
As to whether or not he might be *someone*

A few beers too, don't go astray,
I got talking to a Swede,
Told her ABBA were from Sweden!

She replied 'The Irish like to drink a lot',
I admitted the cliché was true,
Later Dave fell asleep at the bus-stop

And Sean went roaring up an almighty tree,
A laughing coloured woman sidled over to me
And this is what she said -

She said *'I'm sad 'cause I got divorced today*
But you guys! - and I see your friend up there –
- You guys made my day!'

Whereupon Dave arose and Sean swung down
from above
And we were all hugging and hugging
And commiserating on her truly sad divorce.

- 1988 -

Seven days of Falling

That this is how the universe works;
- Chance like a fish – the fish of chance
Swimming in the great connecting sea
That stretches from Stockholm's archipelago
To the sun-coast of Lanzarote,

Okay - let me explain, - I'm listening
To *Esbjorn Svensson* – jazz pioneer
On a Lanzarote balcony,
To a plaintive piano's odd incongruent clarity
On account of having read his obituary,

So - I listen and listen to the crystalline sounds
Of '*ballad of the unborn*', '*the well-wisher*'
In this – this fool's paradise undoubtedly,
It's a delicious melancholy, but this is how
The universe works; – we will die, we will all live.

- 2008 -

America

(It's money that matters, in the USA – Randy Newman)

Yeah Seanie, - you did warn me
About a whole bunch of things;
Like jay-walking across the boulevards,
Or on bringing ID for the bars,
And watching out for those dollar bills
All seeming to look the same…

But then you forgot to warn me
About the twenty-per-cent expected tip
Until too late, – hence the subsequent eye-to-eye
Cruise missiles fired my way
From the face of that foxy young barmaid
That were, how best to say, - soooo not launched
From the decks of the USS Cupid!

- 1988 -

Announcement

Originally scheduled of course
To be rolled out in '84,
But now – at long last, happily,
(Due to advances in the necessary technologies
And the cumbersome procedures
Of legislative issues out of the way),
With – by popular demand
Aided by the self-policing of the populace -
Your government is proud to announce
That as of real-time today
Our big-brother programme
Is up and finally watching you.

The picture of Emily Dickinson

There she stares out from the *daguerreotype*
It's not exactly the brave new world of *skype,*
She's not about to give herself away
Through any time-portal window to her day;
She'll remain mythologized, utterly out of range,
- Untouchable oddball, forever unearthly strange,
With that secret stash of poems beneath her bed
Dream-conjured within her storm-bound head
For - amid her societies' stuffed-shirt decorum -
Something in her wouldn't settle for dumb.
Now good shelves hold copies of her 'collected'
Such volumes as she'd never have suspected,
'I'm nobody – she wrote*, - are you nobody too?'*
O, there's a pair of us, Ms. Dickinson! – and true.

- 2020 -

Foster's Avenue - 1981

Skipping the night-class Maths tutorial
I strolled out of the university grounds
And took the long walk down
The unfamiliar length of *Foster's Avenue*,
Wallowing in that surreptitious aloneness,
Past high gateposts and seclusive shrubbery,
As purposeful cars, receding and red-lit,
Swept by on the glistening road,
And I kept going, a shadow under streetlights,
Walking and walking, on and on. Yeah!

- 2020 -

Mis-en-scene

My father sits at the dinner table
Like some riddle of the sphinx,
His mind is entirely elsewhere
It's of something other that he thinks,

He is taken up and pre-occupied,
My presence a mere irrelevant distraction,
In this - my imagined *mis-en-scene,*
Where there's no cut, no take-two, no action!

And life of course, ever marching on,
Becoming clearer with the longer view,
And my father, sitting there at the table,
And I am there, I am sitting there, too.

- 2021 -

Secret Weapon

That pencil-slim torch you carry
You underestimated for far too long,
- That saved you time and time again;

For how else did you get this far?
It guided you through the darkness,
Guided you past near catastrophe,

Even in the merciless Coliseum of dream
It blinded the most fearsome Tiger,
Thwarted the baying mob to silence,

It's your sole secret weapon – respect it!
Even the abyss retreats before it
As you probe its darker corners.

- 1996 -

Soft day thank God

In a park dulled soft with silent rain
I mull things over and over again
That are long past, and beyond explain,

'Established thought patterns' – the experts say,
Persistences of memory seeming set in clay,
Albeit dampened on this rain-stilled day,

It's a tender mercy I belatedly salute!
For does this real-time landscape not refute,
Trump old argument and bygone dispute?

To laugh then simply at this comedy of bother,
Rejoice in putting one foot in front of the other,
And rain on the wind, - balm like no other.

- 2021 -

Better off

Rock stars will wear sun-glasses
To shield themselves from the masses,
From the pointing-out and the stare
'Isn't that so-and-so over there!'
Who'd need the attention or the flack?

Over creamy-topped pints of black
On the worn bar-stools we agree
So much better is anonymity,
Rich perhaps, yes, but famous? – no,
Not much choice, albeit, although…

- 2021 -

Our feathered & furry friends

And as for those prize-winning photographs
Or artful slow-motion nature shots
It does not matter to the subject matter;
- To our feathered or furry friends,
To Owl or Cat or prowling Tiger.

It's not fanciful fame but of things other
They dream, behind bewitching eyes
That our artists ache to capture,
Even the domestic tabby-cat
Harbours some wholly different savour,

Its inherited hunting instincts
Are still positioned, true and intact,
Primal, jungle-juiced, matter-of-fact,
See how - with one dismissive sniff -
It sorts out flesh from plastic.

Three-walled House

A three-walled house can be lived in;
A fault in the foundations did not allow
For a fourth wall which undoubtedly
Would have made the structure complete,
But I've grown a hedge to compensate,
It keeps the worst of the winter out,

A three-walled house can be lived in;
Once you learn what you are about,
There's always an angle to be found
Or a corner the wind does not scour
And, needless to say, in summer
It's not in the least bit stuffy,

A three-walled house can be lived in;
I've mentioned it and she says 'okay'
- That Rome 'wasn't built in a day',
And I'm ever-grateful for the cliché,
A bookshelf too, keeps the night out
And the black cat has decided to stay,

A three-walled house can be lived in;
Dead leaves blow in but I sweep them,
A minute's work can clear the mess,
I've hung a sheet painting from the ceiling,
I can always change the scenery,
From the outside you'd never even guess.

- 2000 -

Icarus adrift

Messed up kid - hey look what you did!
They are talking surreptitiously about you,
Even your own body conspires against you
Since your wings of fancy melted
In the heat of reality's sun,
Now you're *Dylan*'s damning '*Rolling Stone*'
Lights are on yet nobody home,
And it's all your fault
That it's all your fault!
That you fell into the laughing sea
With only your twisted wings to save you.

- 1996 -

College Square – en passant

I'm sitting on a bench in my old College square,
It is now some forty years later,
And – not to put too fine a point on it -
I was not exactly its celebrated great debater,

I was, in point of fact, an abject failure,
But that's neither here nor there,
I'm still sitting on this open bench,
Musing in this memoried College Square

And dreaming up, perchance, lines of poetry,
And how that very notion is a gas!
Given the mental wreck I was back then
Before I discovered the book that saved my ass.

So, I'm sitting on a bench in my old College Square
As some old guy shuffles by on a Zimmer-frame,
Passing the heavenly cherry blossoms,
We know nothing of each other's name,

We do not, in any way, recognise each other,
Are both unburdened by each-other's history,
I'm thinking now, this college - timeless in stone -
Is mere prop, where may begineth - new mystery.

- 2022 -

Heavy artillery

We were colleagues once - it is true,
And now we are complete strangers,
We were nothing like friends – not that I rue,
There was never any such danger,
You are now a figment in my imagination
As I am but a figment in *your* imagination,
And so much water under the bridge,
Years of happenings under the bridge,
And a long way back to days of youth,
That we are strangers is a hard and simple truth
As non-negotiable as this new-age city
With its built-to-last concrete and steel
Invulnerable to all but the heaviest artillery.

- February 2023 -

The bend of time

Old enough now to notice the bend of time,
And - falling away inexorably - those lands
That will not be visited again
Except in odd spells of imagination.
We're on the high seas now, you and me,
The 'you' that used to be me,
The 'me' that used to be you!
We're on the high seas now, and heading
For a land whose shores give little clue,
With only our hard-won hoard of mythologies
To see our Viking Ship sail through.

Mansion by the Sea

'Can you not hear the wind and the sea?'
My wife remarked as we settled for the night
Into our *Spanish Point* coastal B&B,
So, I put my newly-charged hearing aids on
To admit myself back to the world of sound,
To hear the wind roaring around the gables
And farther off, the sea indeed, pound
On rocks that had once doomed an *Armada,*
Making me recall the odd red-brick mansion
We'd spotted earlier from a distance
Extreme on a headland, and I'd wondered
What class of madman could have built it there?
'My kind of madman' – some rogue voice replied
(Which I chose not to share with my old bride).

- May 2022 -

The Chef

The Chef – it must be said - is certainly
An absolute wizard in the kitchen
And when he's concluded his wizardry
Theres a trail of destruction in the kitchen,
The sink resembling a disaster zone!
Choc-a-bloc with unwashed pots and pans
Mixing bowls and all sorts of utensils,
Blocked with discarded bits of vegetables,
Swimming in sauces and greases…
Someone soon will have to come along
And clean it all up somehow,
Before the next display of the master Chef's
Undoubted and undisputed wizardry.

The Highway

'without deviation progress is not possible' - Frank Zappa

I thought I had found the highway;
Only to find *mein nemesis* was blocking the highway,
I could not proceed down the highway
So had to temporarily detour from the highway
Into the dark forests skirting the highway
Eventually I re-discovered the highway,
Months and months later re-discovered the highway,
Having read book upon book about the highway
Remembering 'n*o man can stop another's journey
down the highway'*
And other miscellaneous quotes about the highway,
Immersed myself in multitudinous mythologies of
the highway,
Continued tentatively on down the highway
By means of occasional detours and cul-de-sacs off
the highway,
Occasionally looking back down the sheer length and
distance of the highway,
At long-gone ghosts still scattered along the edge of
the highway,
Mere gaseous ghosts on the highway,
Gotta '*keep-on-keepin-on'* down the highway,
Listening to shanty songs to stay in the true spirit of
the highway,
- the life-giving spirit of the highway.

Come a long way

We've come quite a long long way
From the spiked ball-and-chain
Taut on its death-bringing radius,
We've come a long long way
From the ancient Viking pointed axe
And beserkers bloody battle rites,
From Norman bow and arrow
And medieval poison-tipped spike,
From indiscriminate world-war cannon
And blunderbuss
To remote drone precision strike…

But then, on the positive side - never fear,
We've discovered penicillin,
X-rays and magnetic imaging
To pinpoint unseen damaging,
Not to mention our miraculous advances
In prosthetic limbs – take a look!
- Just a year ago it seemed
That soldier would never walk again!

Beckettian

A fanlight is lit from an interior hall
Whereupon a great Georgian door opens
And next, there's a kerfuffle and a clattering
As a shabby-coated figure comes sliding
And tumbling down the high stone steps
Onto an ill-lit street, the heavy door
Slams, and as soon, opens once more
With a 'good riddance' or something similar
And a derby hat sails through the air
Before the door slams - this time finally,
As the unfortunate fellow painstakingly
Gathers himself, retrieves his hat,
Dusts off, limping round the corner and away
With more dignity than most might muster,
For they may take the roof over his head
Though never that migrant imagination.

Playing it safe

The goalmouth had frozen solid in the January air
And Kearney in mid-field's *'get it out of there!'*
With a vapoured bellowing, then the ball booted high
Not before reddening Murphy's goose-flesh thigh,
And Byrne and Connolly, they were tackling hard,
And not many people got past big Ollie Ward,
That goal-keeping spot would have suited me best
But Smithy it was, shouted loudest for that vest,
So I stayed out of trouble, way on the wing
And never got the ball, not a sniff of the thing,
My centre of gravity not ideal for football
And impetuous I was not, - in any way at all,
Sub-consciously staying away from all physical harm
Just kept on running to keep my limbs warm.

- 1990 -

Meanwhile

Meanwhile the clocks are ticking
And the sap and the insects are sticking
Under the tree to the car windscreen
That recently was all polished and clean,

Meanwhile - an ongoing war in the East
And new movie out about the number of the beast,
But the end of the world has often been *nigh*,
We'll not be the first nor the last ones to sigh.

Some philosophise that time is not linear
And yet the clocks keep ticking – go figure,
Except that cheap watch I brought in a flea-market
I use now merely as a bracelet,

Meanwhile back at the proverbial ranch
New leaves are fast growing on the tree branch
Just like they did at the same time last year,
Another chance for you and me, my dear?

Conversation with a Cat

Yes, I do have occasional conversations with the cat,
Oh - just a brief and informal chat,
(Its next-door's - though we have an understanding)
It blinks ever sagely – is never demanding,
Electing as always to keep good council,
I know by now it's ever on the level,
Perchance distracted by a passing bird or bee,
And yawning on occasion (though not surreptitiously),
Affecting nothing and patient as a sunrise,
With just a wizened scrunching of its eyes
Signalling appreciation of our exchange - this cat,
Before we part company, - leave things at that.

Mirror-ball

A crowded room reflecting on the suspended
mirror-ball,
Throwing an entire galaxy onto the ceiling
Of blacks, whites, pinks, yellows, every hue,
And all transformed - whether dancing or standing,
You cannot see - but please have little doubt
You are there, somewhere, - and transformed too.

Moving swiftly on to the weather

In many of our country farmyard sheds
Dogs tear new-born kittens to shreds
Which may tell you all you need to know
Except if it will rain or snow,
- For that we have our satellite stations
With a weather eye out for all the nations,
And cameras that can zoom on a farmhouse mat
Where a dead mouse was left by the cat,
(What goes around, comes around, you know)
The sky looks like it wants to snow.

Dachau

So - we took the train out to *Dachau,*
Albeit - the regular tourist train,
Not *that* train of course,
Of course not *that* train!
On a grey day like today,
On a grey day like today,
Not that 1944 human cattle-train,
- Rusty wheels screeching out a rhythm
Monstrous infantility, monstrous infantility.

- 1988 -

Today

Today you'll continue your journey
By keeping at least one hand on the wheel,
Today you'll reach your destination,
Nothing in the past can steal,

Today's events will depend on *you,*
They will go without a hitch,
Today is in your steering hand
That keeps you away from the ditch,

Today is the living breathing proof
Of the exam you did not (after-all) fail,
The envious demons of the past
Now can only pale

Being outshone by today's sunshine,
Never were they more obscure,
These passe ghosts without substance,
No - today's the stuff! - for sure,

For it's another day! – and you are in it,
It would be nothing without you!
Your bones and hormones, mind and memory,
It would be nothing at all without you!

Motion passed

The deputies in the house of the people
Reached the unanimous and undisputed agreement
That the geometric shapes of the circle and square
Be henceforth regarded as equal,
The required amendment to the laws of geometry
(With a provision for the mechanical exemption
Known as the 'square wheel' clause
For designated listed machineries and vehicles)
Was duly passed by a landslide vote
With the required quorum of deputies present,
Before being presented to the President
Who posed for photographs before signing into law.

Ghosts

Ghosts, of course, *are* totally real,
Albeit lacking in the everyday
Tangibility we take for granted,
Invariably they take years to form
And *that* is their quintessential essence,
- Their former physical blueprint being
Long departed - whether living or dead,
Leaving a quite subjective spectre
That may appear on repeat to you
And you alone. Insistent and yet
Physically harmless, they lodge
Rent-free in your mental mansion,
It's true they cannot enforce their stay
In any real or tangible way,
Or impede your path of progress,
Though occasionally they will need telling
In an alarmingly audible voice.

Fine

The *Titanic* too, looked fine,
The damage invisible
Beneath its waterline,

Though something wasn't quite right,
And the iceberg – the iceberg?
- Long gone out of sight.

Existential

I walk through the deserted municipal park
Unaccountably just a little bit nervous
As the scene glides idly by
Like a slow-panning camera
To the left and to the right of me
In the silence and the sun,
Like some movie - a French existentialist one
Whose director, it's been rumoured
Has absconded, walked off set,
And perhaps has abandoned altogether…

When

When journalists are only in it for the laugh,
And the kids busy worshipping some golden calf,
And the pigs take over at the animal farm,
What's left loose but the psychopath's charm?
For nature - they say - will abhor a vacuum,
And the dancing elephant that's there in the room
Can't be mentioned now or anytime soon,
And the oblivious moon still eternally bored
By the earth's rat-race inhabitant herd,
Who may then shift the needle in the groove?
Who is it most has got something big to prove?
And who will benefit in the longest haul?
Who, with will-to-power, dares win, and take it all.

Le Crotoy

Sur la plage tout-le-monde
Stroll with their little pets,
Le Crotoy beach is quite splendid
Except no sign for *les toilettes*

And in the town's cafes
It's *'seulement pour le clientele*!'
So unless you're rather candid
Order *café au lait* as well.

- 2003 -

Mont San Victoire

'Mont San Victoire'
Big in the repertoire
Of *Paul Cezanne*
Who apparently painted it
Over and over again.
Did he ever climb? - I dunno,
He certainly painted it 'just so'
And I should know,
Having inspected it many a time
On the hospital corridor
Walking to and fro.

- 2014 -

Twenty years on

Its twenty years on
Since the terrible day
Of burning and dust,
Of unthinkable
Vertiginous voids…

Twenty years on;
At least its all over,
And normality restored,
And this is perhaps
How God's mercy works.

9/11/21

Butcher

Reinhart Heydrich, 'butcher of Prague'
Riding in the warm esteem of Hitler,
And master of all he surveyed
From his fortress castle on the hill,
Accompanied, he is driven open-top
Through the fear-emptied streets,
It is 27th May and much to be done
For time is forever of the essence
For this most practical of men
Whose mind – away from his inspiring
Draft speeches on national Socialism -
Has often been known to elevate
To the finest appreciation of Opera…

Waiting for the Sun

Where was I back then?
I guess I was 'off grid'
Dis-connected somewhat
In such a meagre climate,
Though powered somehow
By some God-knows-what
Invisible solar panel,
As *The Doors* chanted
Waiting for the Sun
And similar stuff
That for a time, was enough.
Indeed you may know it,
- that very self-same song,
'Now that spring has come'
No? – oh never-mind.

- July 2017 -

Black Cat – Lanzarote

A black cat came un-mewing
In the Lanzarote night
Where I sat with my coffee
(High palms swaying in moon-light)
And I offered it a biscuit
And it sniffed the biscuit
But did not take the biscuit,
Wanting it seemed 'the real thing'
- Did that mean meat?
But I had no meat
So - stretching its claws
Against the base of a tree -
It yawned and slunk unhurried
Across the sun-deserted terrace,
De-Nada – the unruffled
Body language seeming to say.
De Nada.

(2008)

Say no more!

(Humorous poems)

Message from the President

I must tell you, my people – I can confirm
We have, this very day, found *other beings*
Repeat – *other beings* – in our universe
Similar in structure and size to ourselves
And though I say this with regret
A decision has been taken to terminate them
Using long-range thermo-nuclear warheads
Due to their dangerously superior intelligence
Estimated to be 43 times greater than our own
Posing – as one can easily project –
A very real threat to our galactic mission.
Also, their evident distain of our culture
(From *Beyonce* to *The Beatles* to *McDonalds*)
All of which bodes ill for our mission of goodwill,
This alien aloofness and un-human sang-froid
Combined with their obvious lack of weaponry
Makes it an easy and executable decision,
Albeit – as I've stated – a regrettable one.

Nevertheless, our space mission will press on
For it's only a matter of time before we again
Discover life-forms other than our own,
And indeed - who knows – next time
Maybe we can do business; - God-bless.

No way Jose!

This is the story of Lone man Neville
With his gun he never shot anyone
But once hit a man with a shovel

Or so they say,
On his head made a dent – (an acci-dent),
Whatever, either way

The same Lone man Neville
Moved to Utah like an out-of-state outlaw,
Just running with the devil

The local all know him alas
On account of the amount
Of visible cleavage of ass

(But we'll let that pass),
Now he lives up on a hill, never pays a bill,
Hear what Sherriff Doolittle say…

'Yeah, if yr shootin the breeze or killin time o'day
I wouldn't mention the shovel - for fear of trouble
At the trolley bay,

No way Jose!
Nor – help me Jesus – mention butt cleavage
If I can level – about lone man Neville'.

The show must go on

The high priests of serious
Act ever so Shakespearious
In their beards and flowing robes
And ludicrous head-clothes

Unfortunately, 'handmaid number two'
Is having a fit of the giggles
(Hardly in keeping with the play)
And must duck behind the curtains

This is where 'handmaid number one'
Must step into the breech
And ad-lib unrehearsed replies
To the High-priest Caiaphas

(Who may have triggered the debacle
In the first instance
Due to disastrously mis-pronouncing
The son of Seth – named Annas)

As 'handmaid number two' gets a talking-to
From the irate stage Director
And the high priests of serious
Stay serious.

A right royal Fiddle

When the seventeenth century Stradivarius
Got wrapped round the neck of old Dreyfuss
The salvage of the said Stradivarius
Became an operation of the utmost delicacy
With an indignant and red-faced Dreyfuss
Playing second fiddle to the Stradivarius
For - guess which one was deemed priceless?
Not the hard-necked bank manager Dreyfuss
But indeed, the afore-mentioned Stradivarius,
A universal deafness greeting his protestations of
'hello! – I've just been clobbered with a Cello!'

As to exact circumstances – who's to know?
Only that Dreyfuss had it coming to him
And it seems, richly deserved the blow,
Albeit a costly one, being from said Stradivarius
The beneficiaries in the case being multi-various
From Doctors, Lawyers, Surgeons, etcetera,
And old Dreyfuss himself, set to sue,
So, everyone a winner, even the culprit
Declaring he'd 'never heard a sweeter note'
And 'something he'd always wanted to do'
- To crown his bank manager with a Stradivarius.

PSSDD

Yes – that was the crucial and unfortunate day
I shook some salt into my *Cappuccino*
Instead of sugar,
Accidentally – by accident, you understand,
(The salt sure seemed like sugar – so it did)
And my Cappuccino sure tasted (no surprise)
Unsubtly of salt,
This may all seem trivial or mundane
And I agree – to a degree,
And unworthy of dissertation or intellectual melee
Except my taste-buds were rather traumatized
And I realize now, may be suffering
A chronic case of PSSDD
(Post salt-for-sugar dismay disorder)
Not so easy to 'shake-off' - as it were,
So now I check before I shake the salt,
Then the sugar again,
Then the salt, then the sugar,
And once more the salt,
Before I double-check it all again
Just to be sugar – I mean sure.
Every time.

Instant Poirot

Viscount Anthony Mandalay Marsh-Mallowe
Had committed the perfect crime - so he thought,
Disposing of his dull wife Ernestina in a shallow
Grave, except as it happened, one Hercule Poirot
The retired but still brain-active detective
Was holidaying in a nearby rented cottage
(Quell chance, quell bon chance!)
And smelt the proverbial rat annoying his nostrils
Upon spotting the same Mandalay Marsh-Mallowe
Making free with a young maid of the mansion
And especially when the estate gardener's dog
Unearthed items of Ernestina's clothing
And she supposedly gone excavating to Egypt!
Not to mention the great Grandfather clock
Stopped by a lightning bolt at the time in question
And having been surreptitiously repaired
As proven by Poirot upon a visit to the repair-shop
By hypnotizing the watchful Watchmaker
With one of the Watchmaker's own time-pieces!
Leaving his side-kick Hastings to gasp
'I say Poirot! – you've rather done it again!'
As Poirot modestly credits 'the little grey cells'
Without mentioning that they are entirely his own,
Before quipping cryptically to his fazed comrade
'Mon ami – there is always a Spaniel in the works!'

Titanic Blues

I've got the Titanic blues,
I've got the Titanic blues
Looking for a lifeboat I can use,

Heard the scraping on the bow
Ten or twenty years ago now,
Too much *Pink Floyd*, too much drinking?
Time like the Titanic sinking.

Let's throw a party on the deck,
What the hell, what the feck!
Anyone know a Titanic joke?

I've got the Titanic blues,
Where did I get these concrete shoes?
With these concrete shoes
Can't even dance the Titanic blues,

And then the party's over
Save for the orchestra,
Will some tomorrow come like the *Carpathia*?

What is it we should be thinking?
Monday morning wake up blinking,
Get up, get on yer walking shoes
Off down the road with yer Titanic blues!

Some Tournament!

The hush and hum at *Lavery's*
With the pool-room closing
Or about to – with the rider
'Lights on until the decider
Final frame be finished!'
With just three balls remaining
- a stripe, the black and the cue,
And a tension you could cut in two
With Nolly on a mission
But Derek in pole position
And then! – Ado's trailing sleeve
That may- some did believe
Have brushed the black in passing?
Shifting it a quarter inch
Yet still it was no cinch…
Holy controversy! vagaries of pool!
But no time to debate the rule
With the Barman closing in
And Derek went on to win
By the hand of God
(Or – the hand of Heineken).

(Belfast 2008)

Seasick Viking

Do spare a thought for the sea-sick Viking,
Try in fact, to imagine a seasick Viking
For they suffered sea-sickness too,
So, spare a little empathy for Eric
Even if it was a thousand years ago,
(A bit of a loner, he - in Gods truth
Since the cruel battle-death of his father),
Visualize now as he heaves his guts
Somewhere on the relentless *North Sea*
And his oarsmen laugh and laugh, and he
To save face must feign some laughter too,
Inwardly beseeching the Gods for dry land
Or *Valhalla* itself, which in that moment
Must feel like one and the same.

Only Rock-n-Roll

A wolf-whistle howl of electric guitar
Un-reconstructed men pose by a red vintage car
Announcing '*Sharp-dressed man*' and lady '*Legs*'
On the sidewalk passing,
Cranked up full volume – a rock riff cookin'
And the tres hombres of *ZZ Top*
Just standing there,
- Beards grown long from lookin'.

The meaning of life

'Useless to think you'll capture it'
Wrote Seamus Heaney of the Swans
Reflecting on a still-water lake,
And yes, so much depends
Upon a red wheel-barrow,
Yes indeedy – a red wheel-barrow,
- Do google that rarefied reference my friend
But don't go off now
On some great big tangential tangent
On that infinite information highway
And never come back again,
- So yes, so much depends
On one casual defensive mistake
With *Ronaldo* on the penalty spot,
(The goalkeeper guessing wrong - or not)
Either way the crowd is roaring
Like *The Beatles* at *Shea Stadium*
And I'd love to turn you on but you're
Snoring.

Something stupid this way comes

'Something stupid this way comes!'
Got a mixed critical reception at the *Palme d'Or*,
'Estupenda!' raved the Mexican press
On the film depicting an American invasion
Of their native country, whereas the LA Times
Headlined 'What kind of stupid is this?'
And the New York Post commented with a pithy
'This is just dumb', whilst the Times considered
'The problem here is it isn't stupid enough!'
The Southern Star being arguably more favourable
Albeit with an ambiguous 'don't see no stupid here!'
The Director Hector de Jesus shrugging nonchalant
As he twirled his moustaches and sipped a Margarita
Shrugging 'it's got plenty of boom-boom - Si?'
Referring to its high gun-fire and body-count ratio
And leaving the audiences unsure of his ironic intent.
'And that's his genius – to leave us at our un-ease'
As one young uber-serious film buff enthused,
While a shout of 'Merde de Taureau!' was heard
In the auditorium, but was ignored as a wannabe
Obviously wanting his fifteen seconds of fame.

.

Breakthrough at the Seminar

Professor Cransky of the University of Krakow's
submission
That *'God – expressed as a mathematical concept,*
Equated to the square root of minus one!'
Was met with no little derision
Not to mention bafflement by the boffins;
'What is that crazy cranium on aboot?'
Thundered Professor Standish McGround
Of the University of East Uist,
'I haven't an iota' dead-panned another
'Nor I' agreed another again (the self-same
universally un-noted for his sense of humour),
Then O'Grady – inspired by AI robotry – mused
'Let's for the moment accept Cransky's theory
Without necessarily understanding it to it's fullest'
 But this preposterous postulation,
- This temporal suspension of logic
(a subject itself of an entirely different paper)
Seemed to have an inherent flaw
Or mythical missing link,
Until someone further suggested 'a drink!'
(Amended shortly after to 'several drinks'…)

Chalk-dust

– new poems 2023 -

Chalk-dust

At last I returned that vicious final serve,
I do believe it cleared the net with a swerve,
And abandoned the game, walked off the court
Without looking back, - and continued on forth.
No umpire was in sitting, though I trust
And believe, there was indeed, chalk-dust.

New Year poem

A full moon, pastel yellow and visible
Through January trees stripped bare;
It's quite a picture-postcard set-up
Iconic of this time of year,
- This new year that's kicking off
With the traffic torrents already back
But it's the speedster on the motorbike
Flashing past on wet tarmac
That pulls me out of this reverie
To a *now* that knows of no past,
Yes - it's brand-new business-as-usual
For another year, - mad as the last.

- 4/1/23 -

Troubadour

With your much-battered acoustic guitar
O old and much-travelled troubadour,
And nothing much but a bunch of songs
You wrote to keep the score,

Perchance for that one big break?
And a record deal to your name,
And many surely dreamt that dream
Though yours was a different pain,

So, you played the empty pubs and clubs,
You travelled to foreign soil,
Sang original and old favoured songs,
Found 'happy' for a while,

But nothing seemed to last for long
Now you're living door to door,
Still searching for that perfect number
Though no one's shouting 'more',

And no one thrives on mere thin air,
Who can live on notional pride?
When cold and careless winter comes
How long can you take that ride?

But rave on - troubled troubadour,
Someday-soon we'll see your star,
Brightening in a bunch of songs
That tell us who you are.

Strange alchemies

Never-mind that Cupid's mythologized arrow
Inevitably may have missed some hearts,
Never-mind the many great pop songs
That never found a place in the charts,

So many things will go un-heralded,
Diamonds are diamonds because they're rare,
The dice rolls and time betimes unfolds
Strange alchemies, we somehow get to share.

Greystones revisit

For Florence

Alone at Greystones watching the swell of the sea,
Thinking profound thoughts, albeit sub-consciously
Or not, – call it some kind of half-baked plan,
For I'm a poet you see, some class of writing man,

Yeah – it's a good day for rambling & reminiscing,
Good choices made – is why I'm here standing,
And thinking of people that have meant a lot to me,
And the writing of others who knew a thing or three,

I look across the landscape – joining dots of memory,
They weren't joking about 'a mere drop in the sea',
But I got myself to here by hook or by crook,
Sorry to bore - but I know just what it took,

So, I walk on and on towards tomorrow's next bend,
- Forget about the beginning, forget about the end -
And smile of my love - temporarily absent this hour,
My other half, - am raised again to her power….

4/7/23

Near, far away

You really don't have to go too far,
To sun-kissed Lanzarote or exotic Zanzibar,
No need to adrenalize at the horse races,
There are equally as interesting places
Like *Le Fanu Park* in *Ballyer,*
Yes – you read that right, good Sir!
Not most people's choice as a rule,
Yet I am happy here as any fool,
Not most people's go-to, I'll admit
But it felt a kind of natural hit
Where I found myself on a casual stroll
In a breeze as fresh as fifties rock-n-roll,
Less by design than by pure accident
But that was how the day just went,
Killing time around that railed-in Park
(Inadvisable no doubt, after dark),
And bathing in the mystery of mundane houses
Such unknown lives, singles, spouses...
With lives both different yet similar
To my own, (and blue mountains not so far),
Imponderable as any placename on the planet
Today – *Le Fanu Park* - is where I'm on it,
And my own humble and blessed abode
No more than fifteen minutes down the road.

21/8/23

A certain Pub

I note today that it's no longer there,
Long demolished for a department store,
And two of its drinkers long gone, dead,
Where certain things were left half-said,
All now in the churn of memory's
Most unreliable hall of mythic mirrors,
 - it's three-card trick, four-dimensional pratfall,
Whatever – it's always ever all yours to call,
So, no need to feel some half-baked dismay
There's been many and many the better day,
No reason to be perplexed by any of this,
For where are they now, who once took the piss?

Lunar

The very same moon, of course,
That Caeser and Cromwell gazed at
Or perhaps never bothered to gaze at,
The same moon has nevertheless seen
All the storied affairs of men
From Da Gama to Gandhi,
From Magellan to Mandela,
From Aldrin and Armstrong,
Yes - we've put footprints upon
But ownership means nada
In the lunar scale of things,
How pathetic our comings and goings
In the lunar scale of things!
With its reflected light from the sun
Our moon will forever outshine us,
Think what you will - it muses
In its frequent night-time musings,
Think what you will.

Proceed

You might call me a pacifist
And you'd be making no mistake,
Yet there's hands I'll freely admit
I'd never again want to shake,

- I'll tell you that much for nothing
Though I won't elaborate,
The fallout's long been dealt with,
Time's out on that ancient debate,

Still - there's hands I won't ever shake
Though it matters little indeed;
I nod to dualities, contradictions, ironies,
Such words as we need to proceed.

Way to Go

I am just going outside (an abyss)
And may possibly be some time,
Scott of the Antarctic recorded this
As *Oates'* last uttered line

Before he walked into the snow-sheet,
Back turned to the cutting wind,
But what is cold and what is heat
When all reasoning's been thinned?

True - not all worlds end in ice
And not all end in fire,
And to live twice would be nice
Before exhaustion's last desire.

Of one who took against me

Oh – he took against me all right; -
That sudden day of a turbulent youth
When he rode his high horse at height
Wielding his 'three chords and the truth'
Snorting seven cruel kinds of derision
As I toiled with my toxic acres to drain,
Shifting almost immovable boulders
Only night-time reading could explain,
- And never once did he look back,
Not once over self-righteous shoulders,
And I cared – for too too long I cared,
For too long, far too long I cared.

9/23

St. Catherine's Park, April

A stretched-out landscape under a cloud-canopy sky
To a clear precipice of blue horizon, whereby
Imagination tempts to transcend mere topography
It might be a detail from a painting by *Dali*
In the foreground a bounding dog is set in relief
Silhouetted, cartoon-like, a naïve-art motif,
Content to watch the runners - *my* knees alas are
done,
And observing April's first hints of summer sun,
Its strollers, kids on bikes - Sunday afternoon to kill,
So presents the mundane banal, humble of its
miracle.

- 4/23 -

A Grand Canal episode

On a February - Friday afternoon
Having an hour or three to spare
I took myself by the Grand Canal
Perchance to see *Kavanagh*'s chair,

And joined the strollers by those famed banks
Though perhaps not looking too hard,
Recalling some lines but not spotting
The seating monument to the bard,

Only the stock-still stand of a heron
Who surprised then by turning its neck,
For I'd fancied it as an imitation model
But thought it prudent not to check,

Crossing then into Wilton mini-park
And some art installations on view,
It was at that approximate stage
I realized that I needed a loo,

And would have bought a coffee there
If there'd been a facility I could use,
O *Marcel Duchamp* – your porcelain art-piece!
At that moment – my solitary go-to muse!

Away

At Maynooth I take a walk along the Royal Canal
Its high-grass banks and water lilies a la *Monet*,
And, in this sudden still, I think to journal
Something; as the rain that's been promised all day
Adds sporadic droplets onto the sleeping water
In patterned circles to animate the scene
And ducks glide by I'd not noticed earlier
On this sister waterway where *himself* once had been
And wrote from dream-fevered imagination
Would I even think to be inspired otherwise?
But why tangle in needless self-explanation
When the answer is filming through my eyes
These out-of-time moments, this foot-fall'd walk,
Away from the noise of traffic, all the nonsense talk.

(2022)

Songs of the Sea

I doubt the Sea-Captain surmised
'Fellows it's been good to know ya'
And the *Edward Fitzgerald* sinking
In the great lake-sea of Michigan
In the Gordon Lightfoot version,

For a sinking ship is a sinking ship
And not a song-about-a-sinking-ship,
And one fellow is not another fellow
Although 'same boat' you say,
We are all in the same boat,

Or at least, sailing in the one same sea,
And every culture and every creed
Has their shanty songs of the sea,
Their songs of loss and tragedy,
For where else would we be

Without a collective memory
Without some shielding mythology,
Some common connective elegy,
Where else would we be
Without great songs of the sea?

Only rocks remain

Whether of Lord and Lady,
Or indeed of King and Queen,
Only rocks now remain
Where once they had their being,

Only vestiges of a castle,
Stacked stones like a grave,
Whole lives were lived there
That only time forgave,

It's crows that nest there now
In that ruined turret-top,
The summer cars that pass
Rarely bothering to stop,

Whose belted-up back-seat kids
Barely lift an eye
From electronic games
Of dark fantasy.

Getting on

Getting on for old age – or heading there,
Whilst young ones are out strutting their stuff
On the town, in the pubs
And the nightclubs, in the bluff
Of laughter and gossip,
While I settle for Kavanagh's *Shancoduff*
Before I head to bed for sleep,
And that will be sufficient, enough.

For a song

They can take you down
Like a pride of lions,
Elephant memory
Oh - Elephant memory;
They can encircle you,
Laughing like hyenas
As you say your prayers,
Elephant memory
Oh - Elephant memory;
Must this song go on forever
Even though you swore
That it would never,
Elephant memory
Oh - Elephant memory;
Though on the Serengeti plains
No one lives without water,
On the Serengeti plain
It's so hard to explain,
Drink first and then think
About Elephant memory,
Oh - Elephant memory,
Going, going, for a song.

Heading home

Was it a rare
Unguarded moment
Of uncertain surprise?
Just these seconds
Before my eyes
In the stilling night;-
Leaving the supermarket
And heading for home
To find myself moving
Through illuminated leaves
- their dappled shadows
Under streetlight,
Spurring the notion
(Like a bridge over doubt)
Of some 'time-out-of-time'
- That *transcendence*
They used to talk about.

9/23

.

For;   Lorna & Catherine with much love

For;   The unknown reader - whoever you may be….

Author contact pksexton1@gmail.com